THE ULTIMATE SHARK FIELD GUIDE

Applesauce Press is an imprint of
Cider Mill Press Book Publishers
"Where good books are ready for press"
501 Nelson Place
Nashville, Tennessee 37214

cidermillpress.com

Typography: Matchwood, Flood
Image credits: Images on pages 40-41 and 60-61 used under official license from Shutterstock.com. All other images courtesy of Cider Mill Press.

Printed in China

23 24 25 26 27 DSC 8 7 6 5 4

THE ULTIMATE SHARK

FIELD GUIDE

APPLESAUCE PRESS

MY FIELD NOTES

Every good scientist needs a field guide. It's an essential tool for identifying wildlife and telling one species apart from another. Field guides are best used to learn about nature on the go while exploring. The pictures and descriptors make it easier to know what you're looking at. And there are field guides for just about everything, including all kinds of plants, animals, and sea creatures. You can make your own field guides or add on to existing field guides just by taking notes about what you see when you look at different wildlife. What color is it? How big is it? Where did you find it? Recording these details will help you recognize it when you see it again!

There are over 400 species of sharks. They have lived on this planet for 450 million years, and over that time they have evolved into hundreds of highly varied and fascinating species. This field guide will tell you about a few of the most incredible and recognizable species you might encounter if you take a dive into the seven seas.

When you think of a shark, what do you picture? Perhaps you see a sleek, speedy predator, or an insatiable hunter with a frightening mouthful of vicious, jagged teeth. This field guide may change that perspective. Among different shark species, we find an amazing array of variations: sharks that live in fresh water, sharks that emit their own light, sharks with heads shaped like hammers or saws, filter-feeding sharks, sharks that can "walk," and flat sharks that are nearly invisible against the ocean bottom.

One thing that's true of all sharks—living and extinct—is that we have a lot to learn about them. Whether it's through the discovery of new shark fossils, observations of shark behavior, or scientific experiments, researchers continue to study sharks and their remarkable role on Earth. As you dive deeper into the world of sharks, keep your own notes and records about what you learn, so you can become a true shark expert.

Found worldwide in tropical and
temperate waters, close to shore and
into freshwater lakes and rivers

TALL, TRIANGULAR
FIRST DORSAL FIN

BLACK-TIPPED FINS

SMALL SECOND
DORSAL FIN

VERY AGGRESSIVE

BULL SHARK

(CARCHARHINUS LEUCAS)

GRAY ON TOP WITH A WHITE BELLY

From below, the white belly blends in with the bright sunlight on the water, and from above, its dark back blends into the murky water.

HEAVY, STOUT BODY

The bull shark hunts by itself and is relatively solitary, except to mate.

— 11 FEET LONG (3.4 METERS) ⟶

WHALE SHARK

(RHINCODON TYPUS)

TWO DORSAL FINS SET
FAR BACK ON THE BODY

IT HAS OVER 300
ROWS OF TINY
TEETH.

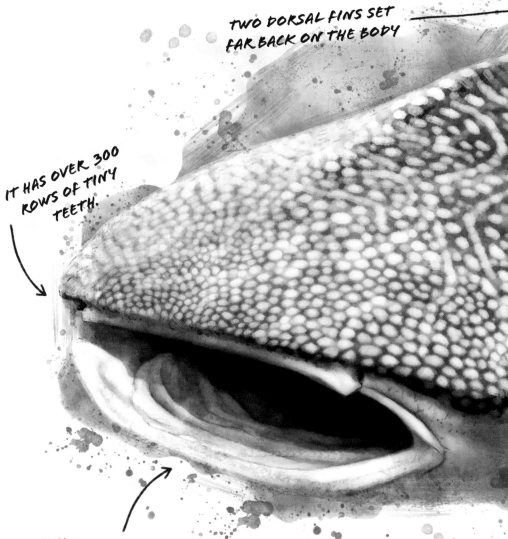

WIDE MOUTH AT THE TIP OF THE HEAD

This shark is a filter feeder. It sucks in huge
amounts of water to engulf plankton, small
fish, squid, and crustaceans.

Found worldwide, mostly
in warm water

**DARK GRAY BODY WITH
GRAY OR WHITE SPOTS
AND STRIPES**

Its spots and stripes are
unique to each individual,
sort of like a fingerprint.

FIVE LARGE PAIRS OF GILLS

The whale shark is the largest living fish in the world.
The largest on record was 40 feet (12 meters) long.

Found worldwide in tropical, coastal waters

The great hammerhead is the largest of
all hammerhead species.

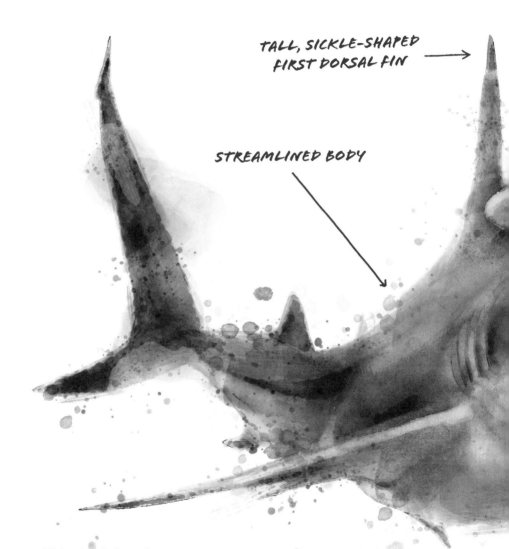

TALL, SICKLE-SHAPED
FIRST DORSAL FIN →

STREAMLINED BODY

This shark has tiny sensory organs on its
snout that detect the electric fields of prey.

← ___ 12–20 FEET LONG _
(3.6–6 METERS)

GREAT HAMMERHEAD

(SPHYRNA MOKARRAN)

EYES AT THE ENDS
OF ITS HEAD

WIDE, PROJECTING HEAD

It will sometimes use the sides
of its head to pin down prey,
including stingrays, squid,
crustaceans, or other sharks.

17 ROWS OF LONG,
SERRATED TEETH

BASKING SHARK

(CETORHINUS MAXIMUS)

Found around the world
in chilly water

**THIS SHARK SWIMS WITH
ITS MOUTH OPEN TO EAT.**

It can suck in 2,000 tons of
seawater and plankton per hour.

MASSIVE MOUTH AND
HUGE JAWS

33 FEET LONG (10 METERS)

This shark is the second-largest
fish in the world.

It basks on the surface of
the water to sun itself.

DERMAL DENTICLES
ON THE SKIN

This shark vertically migrates in deep water.

Found in tropical waters

WHITE-TIPPED FINS

It pulls in huge gulps of water that make its throat expand like a balloon, then it pushes the water out through its gills and traps the plankton inside.

16 FEET LONG (4.9 METERS)

MEGAMOUTH SHARK

(MEGACHASMA PELAGIOS)

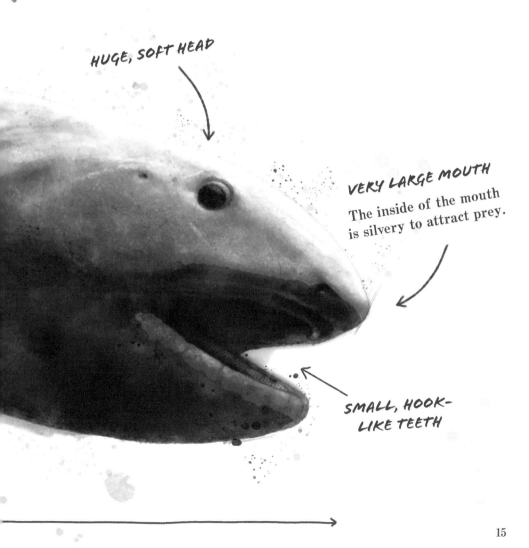

HUGE, SOFT HEAD

VERY LARGE MOUTH

The inside of the mouth is silvery to attract prey.

SMALL, HOOK-LIKE TEETH

SALMON SHARK

(LAMNA DITROPIS)

THIS SHARK HAS BUNDLES OF BLOOD VESSELS THAT KEEP IT WARM.

It can keep its body at the same temperature when in warm and cold water, like warm-blooded mammals can.

It eats salmon, cod, herring, trout, and mackerel.

10 FEET LONG (3 METERS)

Found in the North
Pacific Ocean

THICK, HEAVY BODY

SHORT, BLUNT SNOUT

DARK BLUE, GRAY, OR
BLACK BODY WITH
WHITE UNDERSIDE

This shark is part of the hammerhead family.

SLENDER BODY

NOSTRILS AT THE SIDES OF ITS HEAD

The wide distance between the nostrils may help it locate prey.

← ———— 6 FEET LONG (1.8 METERS) ————

WINGHEAD SHARK

(EUSPHYRA BLOCHII)

Found in northern Australia and southern Asia in shallow, coastal waters

The winghead sniffs out fish, crustaceans, and cephalopods to eat.

LARGE, HAMMER-SHAPED HEAD

Its unique head is nearly half as wide as its total body length.

ZEBRA HORN SHARK

(HETERODONTUS ZEBRA)

RIDGES ON ITS
BLUNT HEAD

Found in northwestern
Australia and eastern Asia
in shallow waters

SMALL, POINTED
FRONT TEETH AND
FLAT, CRUSHING
BACK TEETH

THIS SHARK IS A NOCTURNAL HUNTER.

It rests during the day facing the current and pumps water over its gills to breathe.

Young zebra horns have yellowish stripes, and adults have spots.

LONG, SLENDER BODY

4 FEET LONG (1.2 METERS)

STRONG MOUTH THAT CAN SUCK IN PREY IN ONE GULP

HUGE EYES
Its huge eyes help it see prey in deep, dark water.

MUSCULAR JAWS
It snaps its jaws like a crocodile when removed from the water.

LIGHT OR DARK GRAY BODY WITH WHITE SPOTS

CROCODILE SHARK
(PSEUDOCARCHARIAS KAMOHARAI)

Found worldwide in
tropical waters

**THIS SHARK LIVES AS FAR AS 1,900 FEET
(579 METERS) BELOW THE SURFACE.**

It dives deeper during the day and
comes closer to the surface at night.

— 3 FEET LONG (0.9 METERS) ⟶

NATAL SHYSHARK

(HAPLOBLEPHARUS KISTNASAMYI)

It doesn't like to be approached, which is how it got the name "shyshark."

LONG, CATLIKE EYES

It is part of a group called catsharks.

20 INCHES LONG (51 CENTIMETERS)

Found off the coast of
Durban, South Africa

IT PREFERS
SHALLOW HABITATS.

SMALL BODY
It wriggles into crevices
to hunt for prey.

When threatened, it curls
into a tight ball and covers
its eyes with its tail.

This walking shark is part of the bamboo shark family.

Only two specimens have ever been seen.

LONG TAIL

LEG-LIKE PELVIC AND PECTORAL FINS

Its fins help it move along the bottom of the ocean, and make it look like it's walking!

2 FEET LONG (0.6 METERS)

HALMAHERA BAMBOO SHARK

(HEMISCYLLIUM HALMAHERA)

Found in coral reefs around the island of Halmahera, Indonesia

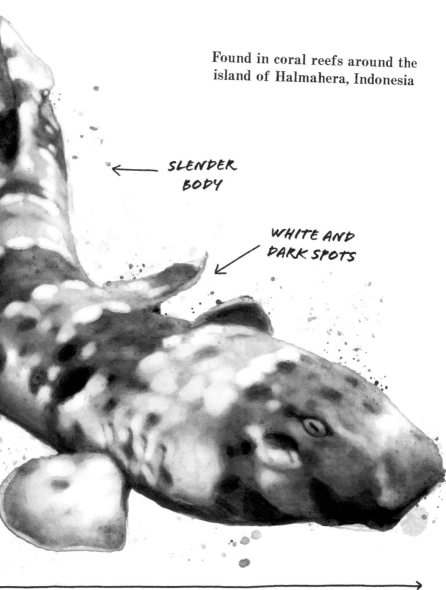

← SLENDER BODY

WHITE AND DARK SPOTS

COOKIECUTTER SHARK
(ISISTIUS BRASILIENSIS)

ITS UNIQUE TEETH LEAVE
A CIRCULAR CHUNK, LIKE
A COOKIE CUTTER.

Since it is so small,
its bite isn't fatal.

LARGE, GREEN
EYES

PLATE OF BLADELIKE
LOWER TEETH

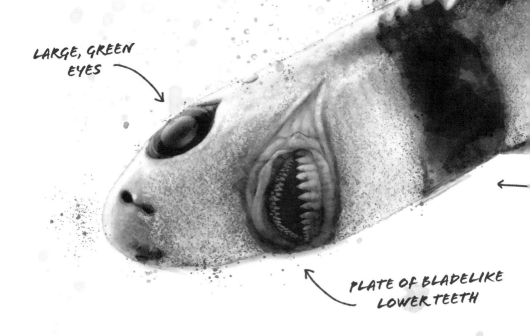

Found around the world in
tropical waters

EMITS A GREEN GLOW
TO ATTRACT PREY

This tiny shark takes bites
out of large fish, dolphins,
and even whales.

DARK, CIRCULAR
MARK AROUND
ITS THROAT

20 INCHES LONG (51 CENTIMETERS)

SARAWAK PYGMY SWELLSHARK

(CEPHALOSCYLLIUM SARAWAKENSIS)

BLOTCHES NEAR THE CENTER OF ITS BACK THAT LOOK LIKE A SADDLE

DARK SPOTS ON SKIN

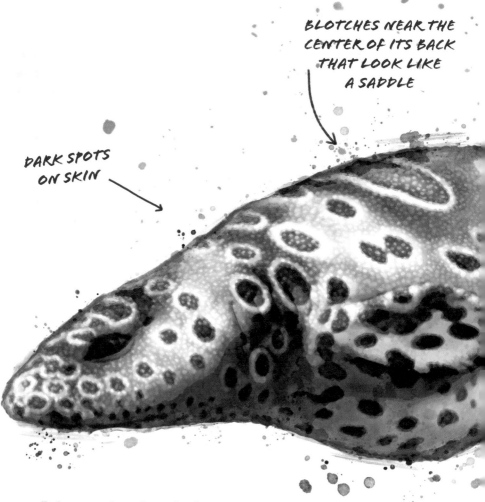

It is a species of catshark.

Found in southern Asia

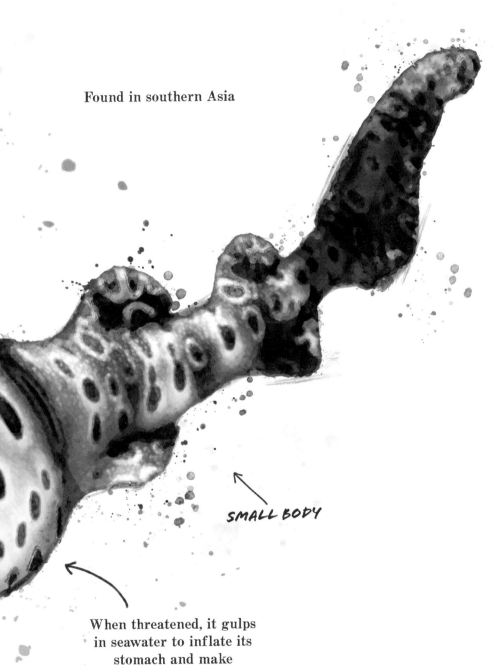

↖ SMALL BODY

When threatened, it gulps
in seawater to inflate its
stomach and make
it look bigger.

15 INCHES LONG (38 CENTIMETERS) ⟶

SMALLEYE PYGMY SHARK

(SQUALIOLUS ALIAE)

EMITS A GLOW
FOR CAMOUFLAGE

SMALL, DARK BODY

8 INCHES LONG (20 CENTIMETERS)

Found in deep water in the western Pacific and Indian Oceans, near continents and islands

It is the smallest species of shark.

WHITE-TIPPED FINS

Light-concealing organs help it blend in with filtered sunlight coming through the water, obscuring its outline and concealing it.

Found worldwide in
temperate oceans

Great white sharks can breach like
whales when chasing prey.

It can dive about 13,000 feet
(3,962 meters) down.

WHITE BELLY

POWERFUL TAIL

TORPEDO-LIKE
BODY

THE GREAT WHITE HUNTS
WITH ITS NOSE.
It can smell a drop of blood in
100 liters of water.

300 TRIANGULAR,
SERRATED TEETH

GREAT WHITE
SHARK

(CARCHARODON CARCHARIAS)

DARK, VERTICAL STRIPES

Found worldwide in warm, coastal waters

It migrates to warmer water in the winter and cooler water in the summer.

POWERFUL BODY

Tiger sharks eat anything—trash, land animals, fish, crustaceans, marine mammals, birds, and other sharks.

IT IS AN AMBUSH PREDATOR.

Its markings help it blend into its surroundings.

20 FEET LONG (6 METERS)

TIGER SHARK
(GALEOCERDO CUVIER)

WIDE HEAD

UNIQUE SIDEWAYS-
POINTING TEETH

DISTINCT BLUE COLOR

It is a fast, graceful swimmer
that flicks its powerful tail
from side to side.

VERY CURIOUS

They have a reputation
for being aggressive,
but sometimes they're
just trying to say hello.

NARROW
PECTORAL FINS

BLUE SHARK

(PRIONACE GLAUCA)

Found worldwide, except
in the coldest oceans

LONG SNOUT

- 12 FEET LONG (3.6 METERS) ────────────→

IT EATS MAHIMAHI, SEA TURTLES, BIRDS, STINGRAYS, SQUID, CRUSTACEANS, AND TUNA.

It will follow tuna-fishing boats
and steal from fishing nets.

VERY LARGE, ROUNDED
FIRST DORSAL FIN

WHITE-TIPPED FINS

OCEANIC WHITETIP SHARK

(CARCHARHINUS LONGIMANUS)

Found in tropical and
subtropical oceans, in open
water near the surface

**POWERFUL, ACTIVE,
AND AGGRESSIVE**

It bites into its meal and
shakes its head to tear off a
piece of flesh.

13 FEET LONG (4 METERS) ⟶

Found in tropical and subtropical waters, near continents and islands

UNIQUE HUNTING METHOD

This shark spins vertically through schools of fish, and when it reaches the surface, it jumps into the air and spins.

WHITE BAND ON THE FLANK

IT IS A VERY FAST SWIMMER.

8 FEET LONG (2.4 METERS)

BLACKTIP SHARK

(CARCHARHINUS LIMBATUS)

IT WILL ENGAGE IN "FEEDING FRENZIES."

If surrounded by lots of prey, it will go wild and bite everything in sight.

← BLACK-TIPPED FINS

GALAPAGOS SHARK

(CARCHARHINUS GALAPAGENSIS)

BROWNISH-GRAY BODY

It will threaten competition away while feeding.

Before it attacks, it arches it back, raises its head, and lowers its tail.

SLENDER, STREAMLINED BODY

12 FEET LONG (3.6 METERS)

Found near tropical and
subtropical islands

CURIOUS AND AGGRESSIVE

It will attack larger sharks, and
can be dangerous to swimmers.

← TALL FIRST
DORSAL FIN

Adult Galapagos sharks
will sometimes eat young
Galapagos sharks.

SEVEN PAIRS OF GILLS

SHARP, JAGGED TOP TEETH
AND WIDE, COMB-SHAPED
BOTTOM TEETH
This shark only has
27–28 teeth in total—
humans have 32!

SINGLE DORSAL FIN
Most sharks have
two dorsal fins.

BROADNOSE SEVENGILL SHARK

(NOTORYNCHUS CEPEDIANUS)

Sometimes it will hunt in a pack to capture larger prey.

BOTH A PREDATOR AND A SCAVENGER

Found close to shore in the Pacific and southern Atlantic Oceans

SAND TIGER SHARK

(CARCHARIAS TAURUS)

GRAY, SPOTTED BODY

This shark sucks in air at the surface to change its buoyancy, which helps it float motionless as it waits for prey.

Unborn sand tiger sharks eat their siblings in the womb.

IT HAS A SYMBIOTIC RELATIONSHIP WITH PILOT FISH.

The pilot fish cleans the shark's gills, which keeps the shark clean and the fish fed.

Found in temperate and
tropical coastal waters

POINTY SNOUT

FIERCE,
NOCTURNAL
HUNTER

— 11 FEET LONG (3.3 METERS) ——→

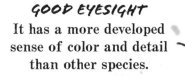

It has a more developed
sense of color and detail
than other species.

It migrates with
the seasons to
warmer water.

**PALE YELLOW OR
BROWNISH BODY**

LEMON SHARK
(NEGAPRION BREVIROSTRIS)

TWO DORSAL FINS OF SIMILAR SIZE

Found in shallow waters off North and South America

Females have a special homing sense that allows them to return to the same nursery area every time they give birth.

It rests on the ocean floor and pumps water through its gills.

11 FEET LONG (3.3 METERS)

It will eat anything, including
fish, squid, crustaceans, barnacles,
starfish, and even garbage.

DARK-TIPPED
FINS

GRAY BODY WITH
WHITE UNDERSIDE

SICKLE-SHAPED
PECTORAL FINS

DUSKY SHARK
(CARCHARHINUS OBSCURUS)

Found in warm oceans, both near
the shore and far offshore

ROUNDED
SNOUT

SHARP, TRIANGULAR,
SERRATED TEETH

It has the strongest bite of
any shark species.

— 12 FEET LONG (3.6 METERS) —————————→

COPPER SHARK
(CARCHARHINUS BRACHYURUS)

Found in warm oceans, both near the shore and far offshore

HOOK-SHAPED TEETH

GOOD EYESIGHT
It relies on its vision and electroreceptors to hunt.

It is part of a family called requiem sharks.

BRONZE WITH OLIVE GREEN
AND GRAY COLORING

Its coloring works like camouflage in different colors of water.

ACTIVE AND FAST-MOVING

Sometimes it leaps fully out of the water.

LONG, WHITE-TIPPED FINS

11 FEET LONG (3.3 METERS)

This shark lies motionless in the mud or sand and ambushes prey.

It is part of a family called angelsharks, but is the only one with those distinct spines.

GRAY, BROWN, AND BLACK COLORING

Its coloring mimics the sandy ocean floor and acts as camouflage.

SAWBACK ANGELSHARK
(SQUATINA ACULEATA)

Found on the ocean floor
off western Africa and in
the Mediterranean sea

ROWS OF LARGE
SPINES DOWN THE
BACK AND SNOUT

— 6 FEET LONG (1.8 METERS) ⟶

ANGELSHARK
(SQUATINA SQUATINA)

IT IS AN AMBUSH PREDATOR.

It partially buries itself in the sand
and waits to pounce on prey.

NEEDLELIKE
TEETH

← 6 FEET LONG (1.8 METERS) →

Found around the
Canary Islands

THIS SHARK IS NOCTURNAL.

It won't move much during the day,
and hunts for bony fish at night.

GRAY, REDDISH, OR
← BROWNISH BODY WITH
BLACK OR WHITE SPOTS

PECTORAL FINS THAT LOOK
← LIKE WINGS

WAVY INDENTATIONS ON THE HEAD

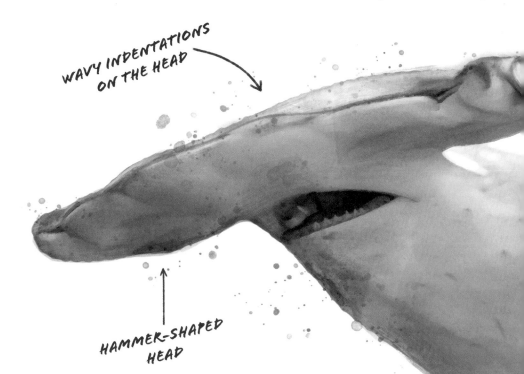

HAMMER-SHAPED HEAD

THIS IS AN ENDANGERED SPECIES.
It is threatened by overfishing for the shark-fin trade.

SCALLOPED HAMMERHEAD
(SPHYRNA LEWINI)

TALL, SLIGHTLY CURVED
FIRST DORSAL FIN

IT FORMS LARGE SCHOOLS.

Young hammerheads do so for protection, and adults do it for social interaction.

Pups stay near the nursery area until they are about two years old, and then they'll venture out to deeper water to join the adults.

TWO SPINELESS
DORSAL FINS

GRAY TO BROWNISH IN COLOR

Its body is very similar in
appearance to the bull shark.

7 FEET LONG (2 METERS)

GANGES SHARK
(GLYPHIS GANGETICUS)

Found in the lower reaches of the
Ganges and Hooghly Rivers of India,
and possibly in nearby rivers

This species is on the Critically
Endangered list in India.

ROUNDED SNOUT

BROAD MOUTH
THAT EXTENDS UP
TOWARD THE EYES

EYES ANGLED SLIGHTLY UPWARD
Its extremely small eyes are
adapted to murky water.

THIS SPECIES IS CRITICALLY ENDANGERED.

It is threatened by extreme overfishing.

GRAY OR BROWN COLORING

It frequents estuaries, river mouths, and mangrove coastlines.

It has sensory organs in the snout to help detect prey.

5 FEET LONG (1.5 METERS)

DAGGERNOSE SHARK

(ISOGOMPHODON OXYRHYNCHUS)

Found in shallow, coastal
waters around northern
South America

LONG, FLAT,
POINTED SNOUT

LARGE,
PADDLE-SHAPED
PECTORAL FINS

STRIPED SMOOTH-HOUND

(MUSTELUS FASCIATUS)

Found near the shore in
Argentina and southern Brazil

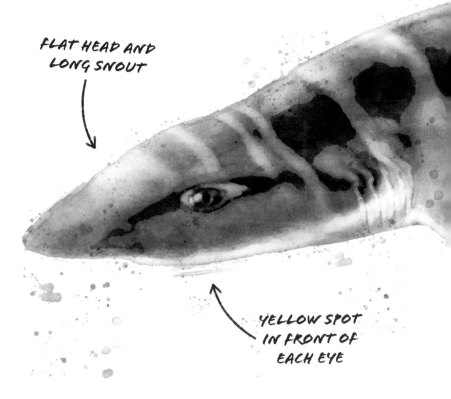

FLAT HEAD AND
LONG SNOUT

YELLOW SPOT
IN FRONT OF
EACH EYE

5 FEET LONG (1.5 METERS)

It is threatened by net fishing close to shore.

DARK, VERTICAL STRIPES

It migrates to shallow waters when pregnant to keep its young safe from predators.

Found in southeastern
Australia on the ocean floor

SHORT SPINES IN FRONT
OF DORSAL FINS

THIS SPECIES IS ENDANGERED.
It is threatened by deepwater
fishermen. Over 80% of the
species has been destroyed.

DUMB GULPER SHARK

(CENTROPHORUS HARRISSONI)

HUGE GREEN EYES
It lives deep underwater in dark, murky water, so its big eyes help it see prey.

It hunts for fish, cephalopods, and crustaceans.

— 3 FEET LONG (0.9 METERS) —————————→

ENDURANCE SWIMMER

It can travel up to 36 miles (57.9 kilometers) a day, and keep that pace for over a month.

Found worldwide, except in very cold water

POWERFUL AND SPEEDY

It can swim up to 44 miles (70.8 kilometers) per hour.

TORPEDO-SHAPED BODY

FORKED TAIL

SHORTFIN MAKO SHARK

(ISURUS OXYRINCHUS)

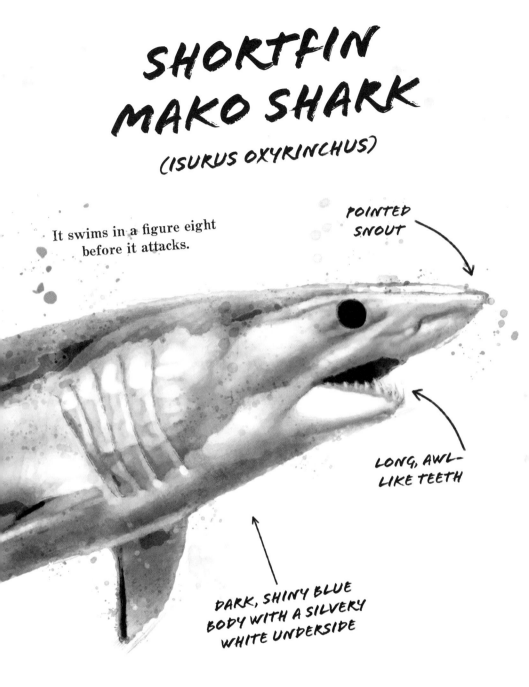

It swims in a figure eight
before it attacks.

POINTED
SNOUT

LONG, AWL-
LIKE TEETH

DARK, SHINY BLUE
BODY WITH A SILVERY
WHITE UNDERSIDE

It jumps out of the water if
threatened, and also to help
dislodge parasites.

— 13 FEET LONG (4 METERS) ⟶

Found in the tropical Indian
and Pacific Oceans in shallow,
coastal waters

It prefers to stay by reefs
and doesn't stray far from
its home territory.

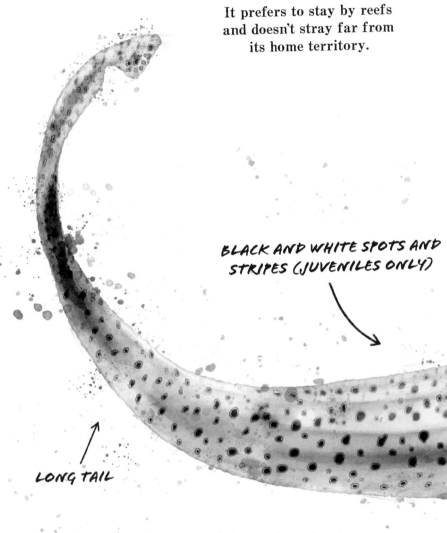

BLACK AND WHITE SPOTS AND
STRIPES (JUVENILES ONLY)

LONG TAIL

It is considered endangered
everywhere but Australia.

ZEBRA SHARK

(STEGOSTOMA FASCIATUM)

SLENDER BODY

They are named for the way they look when they're young. Juveniles are marked with vertical light and dark stripes and spots.

IT LAYS EGGS INSTEAD OF GIVING BIRTH TO LIVE PUPS.

Once hatched, pups are completely independent.

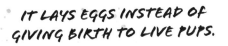

8 FEET LONG (2.4 METERS)

BROADFIN SHARK
(LAMIOPSIS TEMMINCKII)

Found near the shore in
southern Asia

BROAD PECTORAL FINS

THIS IS AN ENDANGERED SPECIES.
It is fished for its meat, fins, and
liver. It is also threatened by
habitat loss.

5.5 FEET LONG (1.7 METERS)

UPPER JAW WITH
SERRATED TEETH

LOWER JAW WITH
SMOOTH, HOOKED TEETH

It eats small fish and
invertebrates.

THIS SPECIES IS LISTED AS VULNERABLE.

It is threatened by overfishing.

Found on muddy and coral bottoms near the coasts of the eastern Atlantic and Mediterranean

It eats marine worms, crabs, snails, and the eggs of other sharks and rays.

It pierces leathery egg cases and sucks out the contents.

THICK BODY THAT'S FLAT ON THE BOTTOM

ANGULAR ROUGHSHARK
(OXYNOTUS CENTRINA)

TWO TALL, TRIANGULAR DORSAL FINS

DEEPWATER SHARK

It lives between 1,000 feet (305 meters) and nearly a mile (1.6 kilometers) deep.

3 FEET LONG (0.9 METERS)

THIS SPECIES IS INCREDIBLY RARE.
Only four specimens have ever been studied.

DEEPWATER SHARK
It lives 1,500 feet (457 meters) deep.

POUCH BEHIND THE PELVIC FINS THAT SECRETES A GLOWING BLUE SUBSTANCE
The glowing substance might be a distraction method to help it escape from predators.

15 INCHES LONG
(38 CENTIMETERS)

Found in the South
Atlantic Ocean

DARK BROWN BODY

NEEDLELIKE
TEETH AND
POWERFUL JAWS

ROUNDED
PECTORAL FINS
EDGED IN WHITE

TAILLIGHT SHARK
(EUPROTOMICROIDES ZANTEDESCHIA)

PORTUGUESE DOGFISH
(CENTROSCYMNUS COELOLEPIS)

FLAT, ROUND DERMAL DENTICLES
The denticles look like the scales of a bony fish.

Found in the coastal Atlantic and Pacific Oceans

This shark is easily confused with kitefin and Greenland sharks.

DEEPWATER SHARK

It lives between 890 and 12,100 feet (271 and 3,688 meters) under the surface.

It is the world's deepest-water shark.

SHARP, GRABBING TEETH ON THE TOP JAW AND FLAT, BLADELIKE TEETH ON THE BOTTOM

BLACK OR BROWNISH COLOR

4 FEET LONG (1.2 METERS)

BROWN AND GRAY
COLORING FOR
CAMOUFLAGE

DEEPWATER SHARK
It lives 2,000 feet
(610 meters) deep.

FEELERS ON THE SNOUT
It uses these feelers to
sense and locate prey
on the seafloor.

2.5 FEET LONG (0.8 METERS)

BAHAMAS SAWSHARK
(PRISTIOPHORUS SCHROEDERI)

Found between Cuba,
Florida, and the Bahamas
on the ocean floor

TEETH IN THE SNOUT
THAT LOOK LIKE A SAW

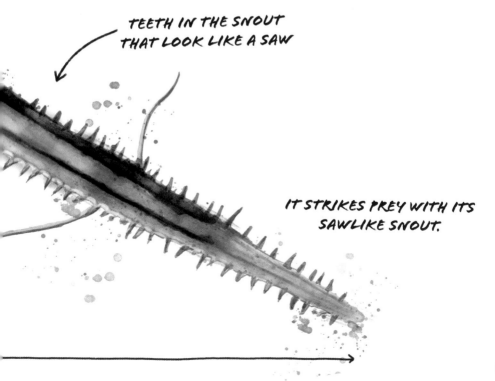

IT STRIKES PREY WITH ITS
SAWLIKE SNOUT.

BRAMBLE SHARK

(ECHINORHINUS BRUCUS)

This is a sluggish species.

VERY SMALL DORSAL FINS FAR BACK ON THE BODY

DEEPWATER SHARK

It lives between 650 and 3,000 feet (198 and 914 meters) down.

10 FEET LONG (3 METERS)

Found worldwide at the slope
of the ocean floor where
continents and islands meet

DARK GRAY, OLIVE,
BLACK, BROWN, OR
PURPLISH COLOR
Its coloring reflects
the light in a way that
makes it look shiny.

42–52 STRONG,
CURVED TEETH

THORNLIKE
DENTICLES ON
THE SKIN

It is the slowest moving
of all shark species.

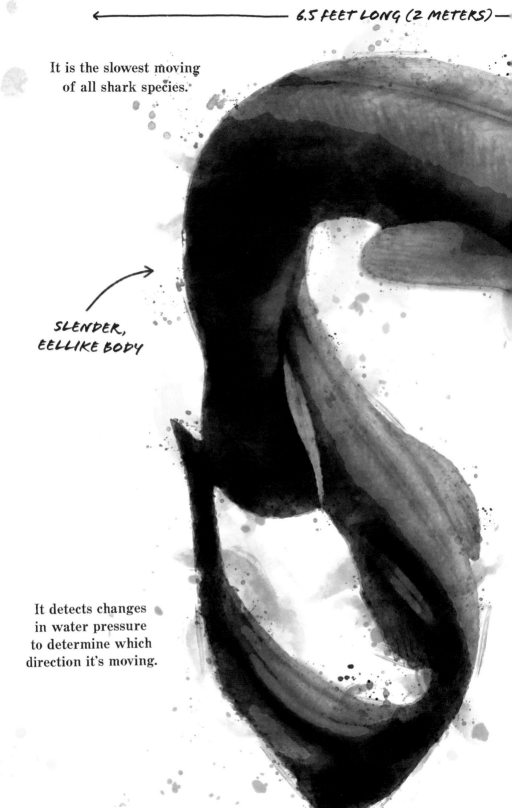

SLENDER,
EELLIKE BODY

It detects changes
in water pressure
to determine which
direction it's moving.

LONG GILL SLITS
THAT LOOK LIKE A
FRILLED COLLAR

Found worldwide in
deep seas

DEEPWATER SHARK

It lives up to 4,300 feet (1,311
meters) down and rarely
comes to the surface.

SIX SETS OF
GILLS

Most sharks have
five sets of gills.

THREE-PRONGED
TEETH

FRILLED SHARK

(CHLAMYDOSELACHUS ANGUINEUS)

VIPER DOGFISH
(TRIGONOGNATHUS KABEYAI)

Found in the Pacific Ocean

DEEPWATER SHARK
It lives between 500 and 1,300
feet (152 and 396 meters) down.

SHARP, NEEDLELIKE
TEETH FOR
GRABBING PREY

It will snatch up prey as big as
half its own size.

EMITS LIGHT
The light prevents predators from
seeing its silhouette by matching
the brightness from the surface.

21 INCHES LONG
(53 CENTIMETERS)

LONG, LOW FIRST DORSAL FIN

SOFT, FLABBY BODY
Its body indicates it is a slow swimmer.

It lurks over the deep ocean floor, waiting for prey.

FALSE CATSHARK

(PSEUDOTRIAKIS MICRODON)

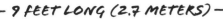

9 FEET LONG (2.7 METERS)

Found off continents and islands

DEEPWATER SHARK

It lives between 700 and 4,900 feet (213 and 1,493 meters) down.

LONG, CATLIKE EYES

200 ROWS OF TEETH

LONG, BLADELIKE SNOUT
Sensory organs in the snout help
it sense prey in the sand.

PROTRUDING JAWS

RUBBERY SKIN
Most sharks have bumpy,
denticle-covered skin.

**PALE GRAY WITH A
PINKISH-WHITE BELLY**

12 FEET LONG (3.6 METERS)

GOBLIN SHARK

(MITSUKURINA OWSTONI)

Found around Japan, California,
Australia, Europe, Africa,
and South America

DEEPWATER SHARK

It lives between 1,000 and
3,000 feet (305 and 914 meters)
down, and probably deeper.

BIRDBEAK DOGFISH

(DEANIA CALCEA)

GROOVED SPINE AT THE FRONT OF EACH DORSAL FIN

It travels in large schools.

LONG SNOUT

LARGE EYES

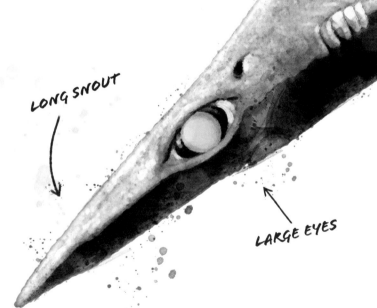

Found where the ocean floor slopes to meet continents and islands

DEEPWATER SHARK

It lives at depths of 1,000 feet (305 meters) to nearly a mile (1.6 kilometers) deep.

It eats deepwater species, such as hatchetfish and scaly dragonfish, that emit a glowing light.

4 FEET LONG (1.2 METERS)

ABOUT APPLESAUCE PRESS

Good ideas ripen with time. From seed to harvest, Applesauce Press crafts books with beautiful designs, creative formats, and kid-friendly information on a variety of topics. Like our parent company, Cider Mill Press Book Publishers, our press bears fruit twice a year, publishing a new crop of titles each spring and fall.

"Where good books are ready for press"
501 Nelson Place
Nashville, Tennessee 37214

cidermillpress.com